What do the Reading Magic Levels Mean?

PreK-Kindergarten

◆ Ages 4-6

◆ Decodable Words — Simple Sentences

◆ High volume of CVC (consonant-vowel-consonant) words

◆ Stories with 150 total words or less

◆ 2-3 lines of text per page; 30 characters or less in each line

◆ Some rhymes

◆ Kindergarten sight words

◆ Best for children who know their alphabet and want to start reading on their own with minimal help.

1st grade

◆ Ages 6-7

◆ High Frequency Words — Complex Sentences

◆ Stories with 500 total words or less

◆ 2-5 lines of text per page; 36 characters or less in each line

◆ Some rhymes

◆ First Grade sight words

◆ Best for children who can generally recognize sight words, high frequency words, and are willing to sound out words on their own.

2nd grade

◆ Ages 7-8

◆ New Vocabulary — Complex Story Structure — Short Paragraphs

◆ Stories with 500-1,000 total words

◆ 5+ lines of text per page; 40 characters or less in each line

◆ Second Grade vocabulary words

◆ Best for children who can read on their own. They read simple sentences with confidence.

ISBN (Paperback): 9798351794785

Praise God

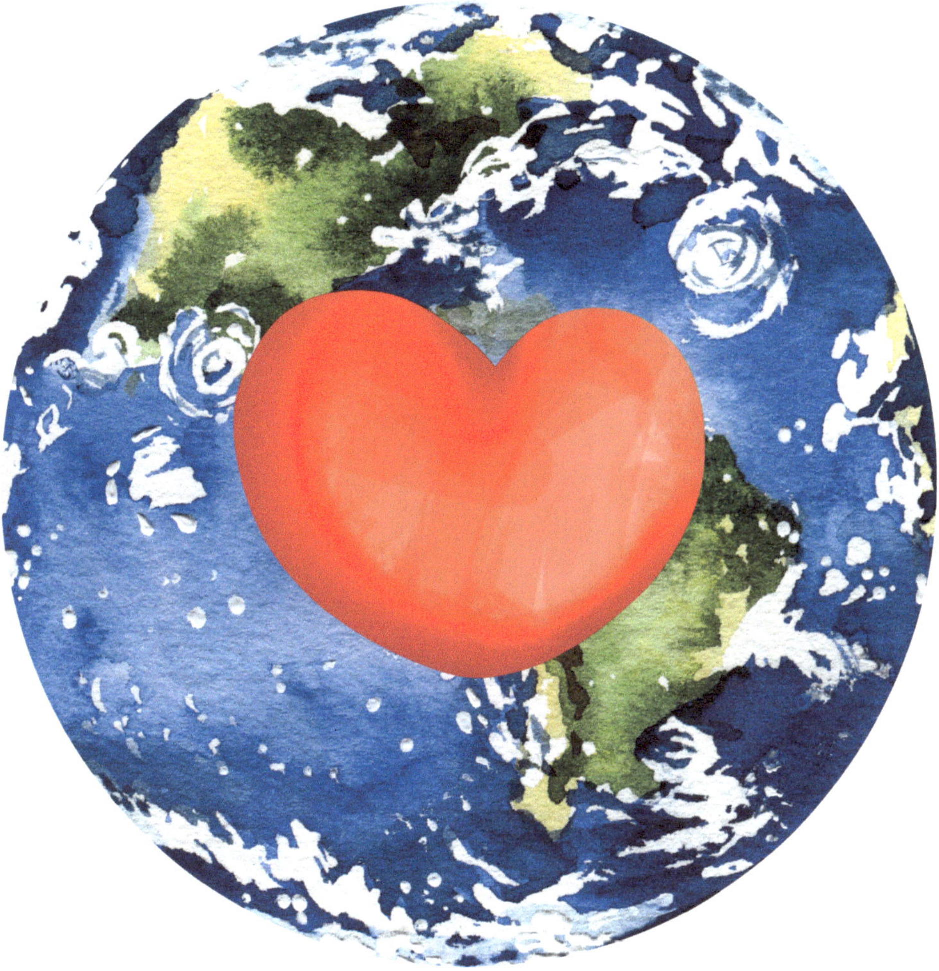

by Beth Hoover

Let the sun

praise God.

Let the moon

praise God.

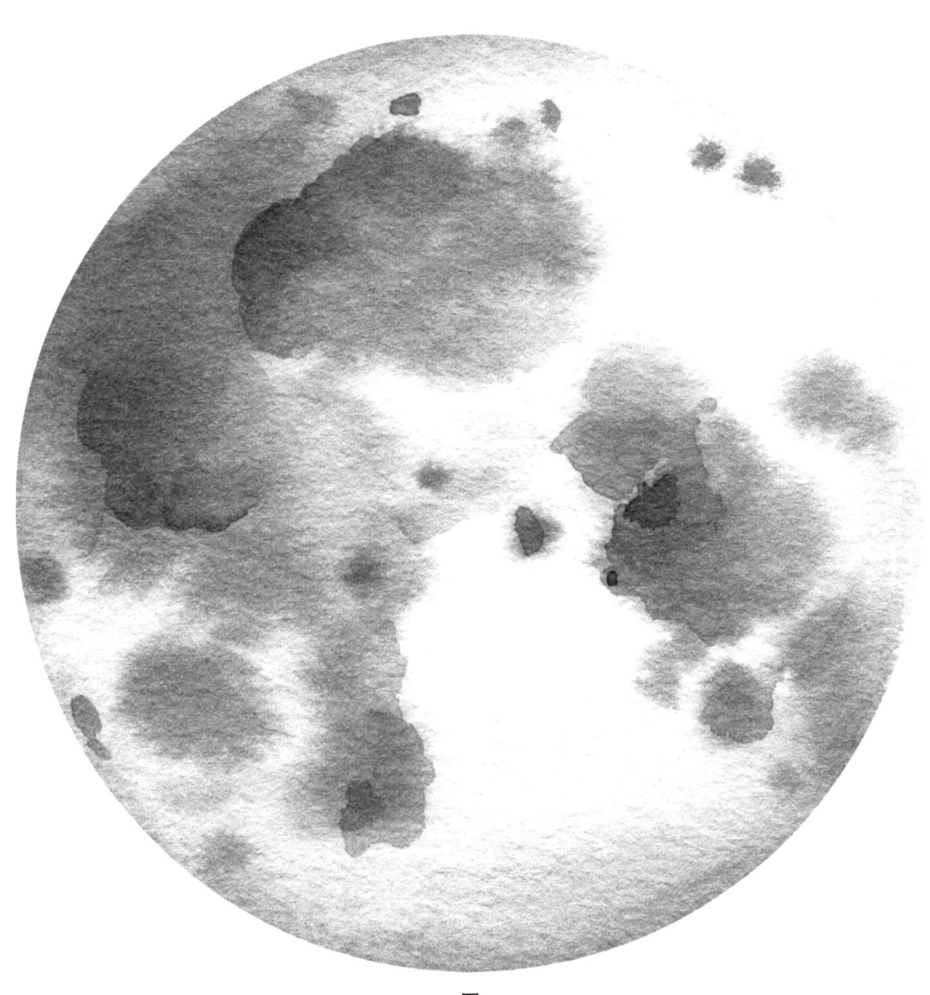

Let the angels

praise God.

Let the planet

praise God.

Let the sky,

the land, and the sea

praise God.

Let whales

praise God.

Let dolphins

praise God.

Let big cats
praise God.

Let bears

praise God.

Let squirrels

praise God.

Let foxes

praise God.

21

Let pet cats
praise God.

Let pet dogs
praise God.

23

Let horses

praise God.

26

Let all birds

praise God.

Young men and women

praise God.

Old men and women
praise God.

Girls and boys

praise God.

Even babies

praise God.

God loves
everything he made.
Praise God!

Homeschool Lesson Plan

Literacy Activity: Poetry

Tell your child(ren) that there are different forms of writing and telling stories. There are fiction books with made up stories. There are non-fiction books that tell stories that really happened. And there poems.

Poems can be made up or based on real events. Poems are different because they don't use sentences in the way fiction or non-fiction stories do.

Poems can rhyme. Poems can have a rhythm, like songs do. Poems can use words that start with the same letter (alliteration). Or poems can repeat words or phrases.

The book you just read is a poem. It repeats the phrase, "praise God." This book was inspired by Psalm 148 in the Bible. Read Psalm 148 with your child(ren). Explain that the psalms are like poems.

Writing Practice: Poetry

Have your child(ren) choose an animal they really like. Write a list of everything they know about that animal. Using that list, help your child(ren) write a poem about that animal.

Craft

Brainstorm with your child(ren) ways that they can praise God (singing, playing an instrument, writing, dancing, etc.).

Using that list, ask your child(ren) to create a poster showing the different ways they can praise God. Children can paint, draw, color, or use images from magazines or the internet to create a collage. Or maybe your child wants to write a play, or sing a song, or choreograph a dance. Let them do what they like best!

Recipe

Praise God Sandwiches

<u>Ingredients</u>

1. Your favorite sandwich makings, such as:

    *   Peanut butter and jelly

    *   Veggies with hummus or mashed avocado

    *   Lunch meat and cheese

    *   Tuna fish salad

2. Lots of different cookie cutters, preferably with animal shapes, human shapes, and plant shapes.

<u>Instructions</u>

Make your favorite sandwiches. Use the cookie cutters to give the sandwiches the various shapes of the things that God has made.

Put all the cut out sandwiches on a big platter. Say a prayer of praise to God. Eat and enjoy!

Maze

Help the baby polar bears find their way back to their mama.

(Answers on page 40.)

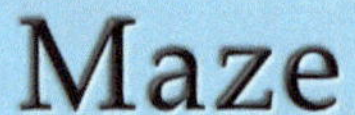

Art
Color the picture below.

Story Recall

Circle the animals that were pictured in the book. (Answers on page 40.)

Beth Hoover doesn't have many hobbies, but she really likes reading. Really. Really, really, really. If you find her with her husband and her adorable son in Montana, she may have her nose stuck in a book. Her husband pokes fun at her because she even reads while she is brushing her teeth.

She will take time out from reading to cook meals (she almost loves eating as much as reading), to play with her young son (dinosaurs are his favorite), to laugh with her husband (he tells the best jokes), or to talk on the phone with her mother or her sisters (she has lots of sisters).

As a full-time mother, wife, and homeschool teacher, her next book might take a while to write. Although, she might just be a slow writer because she's busy reading.

A note from the author:

If you enjoyed this book and you would like to help me out by helping others find it, please leave a review on Amazon! As a self-published author, your review makes a BIG difference to me. Thank you so much!

Answers